The Old Poor Law
1834

D0147322

Second Edition

Prepared for
The Economic History Society by

J. D. MARSHALL, B.Sc.(ECON.), PH.D., F.R. Hist. S.

Reader Emeritus in Regional History
at the University of Lancaster

MACMILLAN

First published 1968
Reprinted 1973, 1977, 1979, 1984
Second Edition 1985

Published by
Higher and Further Education Division
MACMILLAN PUBLISHERS LTD
Houndmills, Basingstoke, Hampshire RG21 2XS
and London
Companies and representatives
throughout the world

Printed in Hong Kong

British Library Cataloguing in Publication Data
Marshall, J.D.
The old poor law 1795–1834,—2nd ed.—
(Studies in economic and social history)
1. Public welfare—England—History—19th
century 2. poor—Services for—England
—History—19th century
I. Title II. Series
362.5'8'0942 HV245
ISBN 0–333–39880–7

Other books by the same author
Furness and the Industrial Revolution (1958; reprinted 1981)
Lancashire (1974)
The Lake Counties from 1830 (1981)

Edited by the same author
The Autobiography of William Stout of Lancaster (1967)
The History of Lancashire County Council (1977)

STUDIES IN ECONOMIC AND SOCIAL HISTORY

This series, specially commissioned by the Economic History Society, provides a guide to the current interpretations of the key themes of economic and social history in which advances have recently been made or in which there has been significant debate.

Originally entitled 'Studies in Economic History', in 1974 the series had its scope extended to include topics in social history, and the new series title, 'Studies in Economic and Social History', signalises this development.

The series gives readers access to the best work done, helps them to draw their own conclusions in major fields of study, and by means of the critical bibliography in each book guides them in the selection of further reading. The aim is to provide a springboard to further work rather than a set of pre-packaged conclusions or short-cuts.

ECONOMIC HISTORY SOCIETY

The Economic History Society, which numbers over 3000 members, publishes the *Economic History Review* four times a year (free to members) and holds an annual conference. Enquiries about membership should be addressed to the Assistant Secretary, Economic History Society, Peterhouse, Cambridge. Full-time students may join the Society at special rates.

STUDIES IN ECONOMIC AND SOCIAL HISTORY

Edited for the Economic History Society by L. A. Clarkson

PUBLISHED

OTHER TITLES ARE IN PREPARATION

Contents

TABLES

Acknowledgements

Special thanks are due to Dr. Dorothy Marshall and Dr. Mark Blaug for their comments on the subject-matter of this book. All views expressed are the author's own.

Editor's Preface

WHEN this series was established in 1968 the first editor, the late Professor M. W. Flinn, laid down three guiding principles. The books should be concerned with important fields of economic history; they should be surveys of the current state of scholarship rather than a vehicle for the specialist views of the authors, and, above all, they were to be introductions to their subject and not 'a set of pre-packaged conclusions'. These aims were admirably fulfilled by Professor Flinn and by his successor, Professor T. C. Smout, who took over the series in 1977. As it passes to its third editor and approaches its third decade, the principles remain the same.

Nevertheless, times change, even though principles do not. The series was launched when the study of economic history was burgeoning and new findings and fresh interpretations were threatening to overwhelm students – and sometimes their teachers. The series has expanded its scope, particularly in the area of social history – although the distinction between 'economic' and 'social' is sometimes hard to recognise and even more difficult to sustain. It has also extended geographically; its roots remain firmly British, but an increasing number of titles is concerned with the economic and social history of the wider world. However, some of the early titles can no longer claim to be introductions to the current state of scholarship; and the discipline as a whole lacks the heady growth of the 1960s and early 1970s. To overcome the first problem a number of new editions, or entirely new works, have been commissioned – some have already appeared. To deal with the second, the aim remains to publish up-to-date introductions to important areas of debate. If the series can demonstrate to students and their teachers the importance of the discipline of economic and social history and excite its further study, it will continue the task so ably begun by its first two editors.

The Queen's University of Belfast   L. A. CLARKSON
General Editor

Introduction

THIS is necessarily a very condensed account of the background to, and the past and present controversies surrounding, those events which led to and influenced the Poor Law Amendment Act of 1834. The latter in turn conditioned the aims, if not always the practice, of the Victorian Poor Law in general. The topic is, therefore, one of primary importance in English social history. It is also one which has been subject to widely differing emphases in interpretation, and which, as regards general agreement, has found no consensus even at the present time.

The following discussion is in effect a guide to the controversies mentioned. It must inevitably take something for granted, and some knowledge of the nature and attributes of the Old Poor Law is assumed. However, it will not be out of place to give a brief account of the main characteristics of this great system of poor relief, which in its practice ranged from the extremes of heartlessness to apparently indiscriminate alms-giving.

The *first*, and perhaps the most important characteristic of the Old Poor Law was that of great reliance on the parish as a unit of government, and, accordingly, on unpaid, non-professional administrators. The small size of the administrative unit meant that its finances were feeble, and that any unusual burden, as in 1815–21, might appear disastrous to those working at parish or county levels. On the other hand, the overseer, contractor, Justice of the Peace or vestryman might appear to reign as a despot over his small territory, and one of the defences of the Poor Law Amendment Act of 1834 has been an argument to the effect that this type of despotism (much favoured by some Tory justices) was swept away. But there is another side to the story, despite the fact that Chartist workers as well as radical Tories united against the Act. It has been argued that the 'face-to-face' relationships of the village or small parish could also lead to greater humanity, and sometimes to more extensive, well-meant and indiscriminate granting of relief to individuals. Parish administration has also been represented as – at its best – the embodiment of a democratic tradition in English life, but that tradition was in reality profoundly modified by the class relationships of the countryside, and those who paid the rates or administered justice tended to call the tune.[1]

The *second* characteristic, connected closely to the first one, was a profound adherence to the tenets, if not always to the practice, of the Poor Law of 1597–1601, and especially of the famous 'Act of Elizabeth' of 1601. This Act was under strong attack in the eighteen hundred and twenties – a consideration which is, in itself, startling testimony to its influence – and it laid down that each parish was to be responsible for the maintenance of its own poor. At the same time the impotent poor were to be maintained and work was to be provided for the able-bodied. Overseers of the poor were to be nominated annually, and a poor-rate levied upon the inhabitants.[2] The underlying governmental motive was that of providing social stability, alleviating discontent, preventing riots and disaffection; at least, this is a fair deduction. The ultimate result of the Old Poor Law was the creation of a vast but rather inefficient system of social welfare, based on the close relationships of the village and hamlet, and roughly adapted to the requirements of English rural society between 1601 and 1750. After this time, population increase, labour mobility and price movements began to occasion much more extensive adjustments to the general system of poor relief, although these were still, in practice, related to the needs of given localities and areas. 'System' is, in any case, a portmanteau word relating to a vast collection of expedients blessed and rationalised by Act of Parliament. The various enactments relating to the Poor Law – they were very numerous[3] –

[1] The best account of parish administration and traditions, outside the massive work of the Webbs, is that by W. E. Tate in *The Parish Chest* (3rd edn., 1960), especially in the Introduction, pp. 1–35.

[2] Relevant portions of this Act of Parliament are quoted verbatim in Bland, Brown and Tawney, *English Economic History: Select Documents* (1914, and later edns.), pp. 380–1.

[3] Tate, *op cit.*, pt. II, chap. III, gives a full account of Poor Law Legislation.

nearly always made reference to, or gave legal expression to, current practice in localities, or to the shifts and variations of opinions in the country at large, i.e. on the part of administrators or governing groups.

This brings us to a *third* characteristic of the Old Poor Law, the tendency to rationalise, repeatedly, what had already been done in practice for a number of years, in localities or generally. Even the immensely important Act of Settlement of 1662 was based on an already recognised principle or principles,[1] while deterrent workhouses, roundsman systems, unions of parishes, and allowances in aid of wages were all known or utilised in given places before, often long before, they became central features of particular enactments or policies.[2] One looks in vain for any fundamentally new idea in the Poor Law Legislation following 1601; rather, the statute book is seen to contain more and more variations on set themes. But the music played by the legislature was not always in the same key, or even in the same idiom, as that understood and appreciated by localities, and it should be remembered that the frequent evidence of legislative expedient and tinkering is indicative of the frequent and recurrent social problems encountered. It is, for obvious reasons, especially undesirable to interpret the history of the Poor Law through lists of Acts of Parliament, there being no guarantee that the contents of the statute book relate in their entirety to what was actually done in many localities. The enactments are useful as a guide to principle only. A *fourth* characteristic, moreover, is the absence of any very consistent body of practice (i.e., as pursued for any length of time) between 1601 and 1834. On the one hand, one can say that

[1] A valuable account of the law and practice relating to settlement is in E. Lipson, *The Economic History of England*, vol. III (1947), pp. 457–69 and 533–5. See also D. Marshall, 'The Old Poor Law', *Economic History Review*, VIII, 1937, p. 43 and *passim*, and the same author, *The English Poor in the Eighteenth Century* (1926).

[2] For examples, see E. M. Hampson in *Victoria County History for Cambs.*, Vol. II, p. 97; J. D. Chambers, *Nottinghamshire in the Eighteenth Century* (2nd edn., 1965), p. 243; S. and B. Webb, *English Poor Law History*: Part I, *The Old Poor Law* (1927), p. 87; Lipson, *op cit.*, III, pp. 479 and 481–2.

the Old Poor Law was inconsistent; on the other, that it was profoundly adaptable! It is of course well known that there were broad shifts of opinion and policy, reflecting social attitudes to the poor themselves. There is a vast difference in the climate of the late seventeenth century, as compared with the general atmosphere of Laud's day, in matters of poor relief, and it may be that the shift towards a greater humanity of outlook in the following century was slowly becoming manifest at a somewhat earlier period than that usually assigned to it, that of the Gilbert Act and Speenhamland. The careful analysis by Professor A. W. Coats would suggest as much.[1] There was a much more demonstrable swing of opinion in the opposite direction between 1815 and 1834. This was the most violent and strongly marked of all, and, of course, it corresponded, in the strength of its movement, to the profundity of the social and economic changes which were taking place. Such violent reactions could not be conducive to sober and careful, still less objective, social analysis.

The study of local history reveals that the overseers of some localities were harsh when their brethren in other parts of the same area were relatively humane, and, indeed, this brings us to an undoubted *fifth* characteristic of the Old Poor Law, geographic variation. It may eventually be shown, however, that these local differences in policy or attitude were not by any means fortuitous; just as the great if somewhat blurred differences between the southern or Speenhamland counties and the northern counties of England corresponded, in the broadest possible terms, to an economic division, so the variation in Poor Law administration as between one part of a county and another has been known to correspond to differences in trade, industry or agriculture. It is in any case inadvisable to isolate the study of the Poor Law from other considerations in economic history. The historical geography of regions and areas, movements in labour migration, changes in agricultural techniques, the destruction of industries – each of these demands examination in relation to the main topic

[1] See A. W. Coats, 'Economic Thought and Poor Law Policy in the Eighteenth Century', *Economic History Review*, 2nd ser., XIII (1960), pp. 39–51.

(and such considerations will naturally affect the position of the latter in a syllabus).

In the period under discussion (1795–1834), the system of poor relief was being more extensively adapted to a rapidly changing social and economic system than at any time in its history. Its administration was in the hands of some 15,000 separate parishes of England and Wales. Very few public men had any precise idea of the true situation throughout these nations, over and beyond one salient fact; it was generally felt that the cost of poor relief was increasing (i.e. for the greater part of this period) on an unprecedented scale. The reaction against the prevailing methods of relief, however, belongs essentially to the years after 1815 and a brief account of those methods will add to the value of the following discussion.

The form of relief most frequently associated with this latter period is that of *allowances in aid of wages*. For practical purposes, such an allowance was a supplement to an earned wage, the amount of the supplement being proportionate to the ruling price of bread, and the total amount of the subsidy being determined by the number of a man's dependants. The original scale, as published by the Speenhamland Justices in 1795, was so arranged that those dependants were enabled to obtain a gallon loaf and a quarter to a gallon loaf and a half a week, while the man himself was to have his wages made up so that he might obtain up to three loaves a week.[1] It is important to recognise that this scale was never given statutory backing, and localities later published their own scales. Nor was relief always given in money; a man might have his wages made up in flour.[2] The fact that the labourer was enabled to add, in some areas and instances, the equivalent of 1s. 6d. to 2s. 6d. a week to his income for the birth of each child has been connected, by some authorities, with the growth of population in areas where the Speenhamland (or allowance) system was adopted. Other students,

[1] A useful account of the Speenhamland scale is in Tate, *op cit.*, pp. 230–1.

[2] This example, given by Sir Frederick Morton Eden in *The State of the Poor* (1797, 1928 abridged edition), p. 195, is from Newton Valence in Hampshire. As local historical research proceeds, it is likely that many other variants of the allowance system will be revealed.

13

however, regard this argument as a *non sequitur*, and, in any case, there has been little sustained investigation into the standards of living and of nutrition implied. It is plain enough, in the light of more general modern knowledge, that both were low. The method of allowances-in-aid-of-wages sprang out of an inflationary crisis in 1795, and was an alternative to, and a method of evading the payment of, a minimum statutory earned wage. Like nearly every other expedient connected with poor relief, it was scarcely a new idea, and local historians encounter it much earlier than the year stated; but not, of course, on a widespread scale nor related so explicitly to the price of wheat or bread.[1] In fact, allowances had many variants, and after 1815 some parishes paid them on a family basis *only* if the number of children exceeded three, while the Speenhamland-type scales were much reduced in many places in the years following 1815. Bread scales *as such* were often unused.

Another expedient adopted was that of the *Labour Rate*. The essence of this system was that a parish rate was levied to cover the relief of the able-bodied unemployed, and that each labourer's services then had a price set on them. A ratepayer might then choose to employ labourers, each at the appropriate amount, or pay the rate – from which he was otherwise excused. If he paid less than the amount representing the assessed wage figure for each labourer, then he had to pay the difference to the parish. Surplus labourers were divided among the ratepayers in proportion to the rates paid by the latter. It is important to stress that the farmer could choose his labourers, and that competition for the services of the best men was allowed to have some play. The system therefore had a positive feature which is sometimes overlooked. It is not known how widespread the Labour Rate became during the wartime years, but extensive data for 1832 suggest that only one parish in five used it, even in the south of England. An even less commonly used system in 1832 was the *Rounds-man system*, whereby able-bodied pauper labourers were offered employment in turn, i.e. by *houserow*, by the farmer-

---

[1] Miss E. M. Hampson, in the *Victoria County History for Cambs.* article cited, points out that 'By the beginning of the eighteenth century grants were sometimes made in Cambridgeshire even to able-bodied men who were "overcharged with children"' (*loc. cit.*).

ratepayers in a parish. The latter paid part of their wages, the parish paying the rest, and to that extent wages were subsidised. This system allowed no competition for labour; there are also indications that the general principle which it embodied had deep roots in the past.

The idea of giving relief, by subsidy or other means, to able-bodied labourers had indeed awakened criticism at a much earlier stage, when the Workhouse or General Act of 1722–3 permitted groups of parishes to build workhouses and to apply the test whereby any person applying for relief had to enter such an institution in order to be relieved. By 1796, however, there had been a total change in policy; overseers and justices were empowered to order outdoor relief without imposing the workhouse test. But it is important to emphasise that this was done in extraordinary circumstances – of widespread distress and even unrest – and also as a logical continuation of humane policies and attitudes which had been slowly evolving. Methods of relief *out* of the workhouse or poorhouse were an accepted and essential part of Poor Law practice, and were a reaction to the increasing numbers of paupers which appeared in parish after parish during the three or four decades before 1796. Most of these paupers were not able-bodied, and they offered too many distinct human problems for even the most constructively-run workhouse to deal with. Miss E. M. Hampson's researches in Cambridgeshire have suggested that despite some promising experiments, few workhouses in that county operated successfully for any length of time, especially when designed as productive establishments.[1] 'Setting the poor on work' was central to the earlier Poor Law tradition, but without crash remedies the policy stood little chance of success in the face of structural unemployment.

Conflicting Views of the Old Poor Law

MUCH of what has been said is uncontroversial, and will be well known to students of economic history. The general

[1] E. M. Hampson, *The Treatment of Poverty in Cambridgeshire* (1934), esp. pp. 72–80, 100–1.

outlines of Poor Law history following 1795 are also well known. The allowance system is believed to have become widespread during the Napoleonic Wars, and, as the Webbs put it, the general adoption of the Speenhamland scale 'met with little criticism so long as the war lasted'.[1] Meanwhile, national expenditure on poor relief reached new and unprecedented levels even in relation to a growing population. The end of the wars brought only temporary alleviation coupled with agricultural 'depression'. The ensuing social and political unrest brought a profound reaction in attitudes to the poor, and there was a marked resurgence of the belief that any kind of charity, over and beyond relief in cases of dire necessity, tended to encourage idleness and vice. Meanwhile, the pressing burden of poor relief appeared to be almost irremovable, and it was ever more fashionably thought that allowances and wage subsidies were root causes of unwanted rural population increase as well as shiftlessness. The general problem of poor relief was examined in a series of parliamentary enquiries, culminating in the Poor Law Commission of 1832–4.

The Webbs, and some recent writers, have seen the findings of this Commission as grossly biased against the then systems of poor relief, including the allowance system. R. H. Tawney went even further and described the final report of the Commissioners as 'brilliant, influential and wildly unhistorical'[2] in view of its assumption that distress was caused by 'individual improvidence and vice'. Since the Tawney–Webb criticisms were uttered, over a generation ago, the controversy has been a shifting one. The editors of a comparatively recent collection of historical documents[3] committed themselves to what they evidently felt was an appropriate retort, pointing out that 'to look at the Report of 1834 in the light of the administrative experience and powers of social analysis gained in the succeeding three-quarters of a century...is unhistorical', and implying that Chadwick and Senior were right to concentrate on the evils of the allowance

[1] S. and B. Webb, *The Old Poor Law* (for fuller reference, see p. 11, n. 2 above), p. 182.
[2] R. H. Tawney, *Religion and the Rise of Capitalism* (Pelican ed., 1938), p. 211.
[3] G. M. Young and W. D. Handcock (ed.), *English Historical Documents, 1833–1874* (1956), p. 684.

system, 'the problem primarily before them'. A still more recent investigator, Dr. Mark Blaug, has gone even further in the opposite direction than R. H. Tawney. After close analysis of the social survey carried out on behalf of the Poor Law Commission, Dr. Blaug has concluded that the Report of 1834 is not only a 'wildly unhistorical' one, but also a 'wildly unstatistical' effusion.[1]

One of Tawney's adjectives, however, would command universal assent among historians. The report was certainly 'influential'. Not only did it affect Poor Law policy right into the twentieth century, despite social analysis; its assumptions, implicit and explicit, have guided historical investigators until the present day, even though the individual conclusions regarding that policy vary from qualified assent to violent dissent. The Commissioners' strictures on the social and economic effects of allowances have, in other words, been taken entirely seriously, and the late Eleanor Rathbone (not a historian but an expert on family allowances) expressed what is undoubtedly a common viewpoint when she dismissed the Speenhamland system because it 'put the idle or inefficient family on the same level with the industrious'.[2] As will be seen, it may well be a mistake to equate the crash remedies of an eighteenth-century agricultural economy with the welfare provisions of modern industrial society, even though, if the Commissioners are to be believed, allowances were spreading, or in danger of spreading, throughout England by 1832. Mark Blaug's arguments, which are now widely known if not uncritically accepted, have, in rationally argued terms, challenged this view more or less completely – and it is not necessary to accept his arguments *in toto* to believe that the threats to social health supposedly implicit in the Old Poor Law were greatly exaggerated, at least in the language and findings of Chadwick, Senior and the members of the Commission generally.

How did this come about? We must consider the topic under two main heads; the nature of the Commissioners' own enquiry, and the nature of the attitudes which seem consistently to have governed and coloured their observations.

[1] Mark Blaug, 'The Poor Law Report Re-examined', *Journal of Economic History*, XXIV (1964), pp. 229–45.
[2] Eleanor Rathbone, *Family Allowances* (1949), p. 10.

The Commission of Enquiry, 1832

STUDENTS of this subject will find a typically thorough account of the circumstances and some of the consequences of the Commission in one of the great studies by the Webbs, *English Poor Law History: The Last Hundred Years*, volume i. The evidence that was set forth by these authors, despite some recent questionings, leaves little doubt that the Commission was influenced, decisively, by utilitarian thought. This body also set about the most detailed social investigation ever undertaken in these isles up to that time. Twenty-six investigators – suspected by the Webbs to be Benthamites! – visited about three thousand townships and parishes throughout England and Wales, mostly in the late months of 1832, in an attempt to find out the relevant details of parish Poor Law administration. The absence of any previously accumulated body of knowledge of equal weight meant that the investigators, the Assistant Commissioners, were assisted greatly by a ready common hypothesis in what might otherwise have been an unmanageable task. This hypothesis, which undoubtedly appeared extremely fruitful, and which therefore seemed to justify itself, was that allowances-plus-indiscriminate-parish-relief were widespread and harmful.

The Assistant Commissioners were aided in their work by an elaborate questionnaire touching on various aspects of the parish economies, relief systems and labour relations. Replies were returned for rather over 10 per cent of the 15,000 parishes of England and Wales, the responding parishes containing about 20 per cent of the total population of the two countries. These were subsequently printed in 'Answers to Rural Queries' and 'Answers to Town Queries', the relevant volumes being of such an unmanageable nature as to deter even researchers like the Webbs. They are in fact immensely valuable sources of local and county economic and social history. In recent years both Blaug (1964) and Williams (1981) have subjected the answers of the parish officers to analysis,[1] and it appears that on the basis of the information available, Mark Blaug was probably right to argue for a

---

[1] Blaug, 'The Poor Law Report Re-examined', 234ff.; K. Williams, *From Pauperism to Poverty* (1981), pp. 147–55.

diminution of the practice of giving child allowances between 1824 and 1832. Huzel (1980) has drawn attention to the abandonment of allowances in sixty parishes, many of them having performed this action in the period specified. This does not of course mean that the Poor Law *ipso facto* 'reformed itself', and according to Williams's calculations, 59 per cent of rural parishes were giving child allowances in 1832. The 'Rural Queries' touching on this subject, which are described by the latter writer, were so involved in their phrasing that it is difficult to know what parish officers made of them, just as it is easy to suspect that the compilers of the Poor Law Commission report (1832) used the answers selectively and with bias.

Any bias – and its existence is surely not in doubt – had the effect of lumping together family allowances as such, paid to a man in receipt of a low wage in respect of the children in his family, and a subsidy, paid out of the rates, in support of a man's wage. This distinction was not seen as a crucial one. It is true that this distinction may seem fundamentally unimportant in the sense that either form of payment could produce heavy additions to local rate burdens, and also true that the Commissioners had attempted, in another set of questions, to distinguish between these types of payment; but they, the Commissioners, produced no comprehensive statistical findings to support their argument that allowances were becoming increasingly widespread. But, in the light of their own hypothesis, it was most important to know how many people were in receipt of family allowances, and in what geographical distribution, and also to know whether the second, third or fourth child in a family qualified for allowance. The precise form of qualification is of much significance, because if the Malthusian argument – that the provision of sustenance for each additional child would lead to an increase in births – had been invoked, the argument was not strong, for, if we accept Mark Blaug's argument, 'the allowances were generally paid for a third, fourth or fifth child, and its amount was related in each parish to the local employment opportunities for children'. Huzel (1980) has taken this argument into the field of rigorous empirical testing, and has shown that, so far, the Malthusian hypothesis

– that scaled parish relief meant production of more children by the poor – simply does not stand up, especially when related to allowances for given numbers of children. Wage or income subsidies, also, may have had little direct relevance to fertility, although a geographical exercise might be pursued.

Chadwick, Senior and their colleagues were not, of course, primarily concerned with the distinction between the forms of relief, and it has therefore been necessary to find the frequency of these modes of payment in two groups of counties, designated 'Speenhamland' and 'Non-Speenhamland', viz. in 1832. For purposes of convenience, a Speenhamland county may be defined as one which the 1824 Committee on Labourers' Wages 'found to be making use of the principle of supplementing earned wages', and eighteen of these, mainly in the South and Midlands, can be identified.[1] In the light of the 1832 returns from parish officers, Dr. Blaug discovered that 'only 11 per cent of the non-Speenhamland counties paid allowances-in-aid-of-wages', i.e. direct wage subsidies as distinct from child or family allowances. The latter, on the other hand, were in common use: 'two out of three Speenhamland counties and one out of three non-Speenhamland counties made such payments', but only a tiny proportion of parishes made payments for the first two children.[2]

In the face of such revelations, the student will naturally ask whether the Commissioners were even aware of what the returns signified. The truth seems to be that their conclusions were impressionistic only, and they relied very heavily on the general views of the Assistant Commissioners, whose surveys occupy much space in the great range of published volumes which finally appeared. On the other hand, Dr. Blaug concedes that the reporting parishes – on the returns from which he bases the startling conclusions outlined – may not

[1] They were Beds., Berks., Bucks., Cambs., Devon, Dorset, Essex, Hunts., Leicester, Norfolk, Northants., Notts., Oxford, Suffolk, Sussex, Warwick, Wilts., and the E. and N. Ridings of Yorks. The N. Riding and Notts. are, to say the least, marginal cases. It is very much to be doubted whether a 'true' Speenhamland county existed for very long, but the concept is useful.
[2] 'The Poor Law Report Re-examined', 238–9.

have 'constituted anything like a random sample of the total number of parishes' in England and Wales. We do not know what basis of selection, if any, was originally used, and, illuminating as modern statistical methods can be, there remains the disquieting possibility that another selection might have given different results. In other respects, however, the results of the analysis of the parish answers run closer to what might be expected, and to that extent carry indications of authenticity or representativeness; e.g., expenditure on the poor did in fact average out at proportionally higher figures in the Speenhamland counties, or their sample parishes, than in the non-Speenhamland examples, and the former were more inclined to employ bread scales, roundsman systems and labour rates than the latter. These stratagems, for long considered essential features of the Old Poor Law, are seen to have had a hold that was marginal or slipping in many areas, and we are sharply reminded that grass-roots research on the original parish documents will be the ultimate arbiter.[1] The drift of the official questionnaires was such that we shall never know, in the absence of this research, when any process of reformation or adaptation had commenced, and Chadwick and Senior were more concerned to know when allowances and wage subsidies had been *instituted* than when they had been abandoned. Dr. Blaug suggests that 'the Speenhamland system had its greatest vogue during the Napoleonic Wars, but the severe strictures of the Committee Reports on the Poor Laws of 1817 and 1818 and the Select Committee on Labourers' Wages of 1824 would seem to have persuaded most of the poor law vestries to do away with it'. In fact, as Dr. Daniel A. Baugh has pointed out (1975), Mark Blaug's argument is very difficult to sustain statistically, for, as the former scholar demonstrates, poor relief in the post-war period was not primarily conditioned by administrative arrangements, but was profoundly influenced by the cost of food, especially wheat. To this extent, any post-war 'abandonment' was accompanied by *rising* real

---

[1] Mark Neuman challenges the other-than-heavily-qualified use of the Speenhamland concept in his essay 'Speenhamland in Berkshire', in Martin (ed.) *Comparative Development in Social Welfare* (1972), pp. 85–127.

costs of poor relief immediately after the war, and if the early twenties are meant, then the gently falling real costs of such relief are hardly dramatic.[1]

In other words, the statistical trends are such that the results of any large-scale administrative upheaval are difficult to detect, if indeed they took effect at all. Dr. Baugh's examples are especially interesting in that they concentrate comprehensively on Kent, Essex and Sussex, and as he indicates, the documentary evidence points in two directions – towards the abandonment of allowances in some localities, and towards their adoption (in the twenties) in others. On balance, he rejects the idea of self-reformation in the parishes of these counties, but methods of relief are not at the root of his argument, which is that poor relief trends were a reflection of food prices, and moved in harmony with them. It followed, then, that 'Speenhamland' and 'non-Speenhamland' counties showed broadly similar movements in relief expenditure.

Yet the mere act of an experimental separation of the two types of county has been of considerable utility – as long as one does not take it too seriously. Mark Blaug's challenge to received views, too, has been invaluable in itself, and has been fruitful in encouraging other empirical investigations. Meanwhile, we shall not forget the original contribution of the real giants, the Webbs, whose view[2] of the bias of the Poor Law Commission is shared by Blaug and many others, even though the work of the Assistant Commissioners calls for more research at the county and local levels. That some of these investigators could display bias is well known, but it is not of course true that they engaged in wholesale *suppressio veri*. They very frequently produced evidence which was not strictly in support of their case. On the other hand, there were also cases of selection of evidence, and this seems to have happened, for example, in Nottinghamshire and

[1] D. A. Baugh, 'The Cost of Poor Relief in South-East England, 1790–1834', *Economic History Review*, 2nd Ser., XXVIII (1975), pp. 50–68.

[2] S. and B. Webb, *English Poor Law History*, Part II; *The Last Hundred Years*, vol. 1 (1929), pp. 82–90.

Dorset.[1] But perhaps it is unhistorical to expect anything in the way of disciplined detachment and objectivity in the conduct of the enquiry of 1832. One of the aims of the Commission, we may remember, was 'to educate public opinion', and Chadwick was hardly the man to maintain a rigid separation of edification on the one hand and cold objectivity on the other. Chadwick and Senior educated opinion so well that the Poor Law Amendment Act of 1834 was in no small measure their own achievement.

The Financial Burden of the Old Poor Law

A scholar could accept all the criticisms of the Poor Law Commission and its enquiry, and yet heartily defend Chadwick for his part in the administrative revolution implied in the Act of 1834. The Old Poor Law looked costly, it was certainly clumsy and often wasteful, and the burden of poor relief did not appear to be shrinking with the years. The New Poor Law took power and initiative out of the hands of the 15,000 separate parishes, and put those attributes in the hands of the central authority and of elected guardians of the poor. It brought in professionalism in administration where there had been amateurism, and it represented an uncompromising (middle-class?) attitude to poverty which may have been unhistorical but which certainly appeared to get things done.

The financial burden had most certainly appeared heavy. Official statistics of this period are regarded, rightly, with some scepticism, but one can assume that these give some idea of the extent of pauperism and the cost of poor relief. The general impression derived from them is that between about 1784 and the years immediately following the termination of

---

[1] J. D. Marshall, 'The Nottinghamshire Reformers and their contribution to the Old Poor Law', *Economic History Review*, XIII (1961), p. 387, n. 3, and p. 395; G. Body, *The Administration of the Poor Law in Dorset, 1760–1834* (Ph.D. thesis in the University of Southampton, 1964). I am indebted to Dr. Dorothy Marshall for details concerning Dr. Body's important study; an Assistant Commissioner in Dorset, for example, a Mr. Okeden, was repeatedly guilty of bias and exaggeration.

the French wars expenditure on the poor rose between two and three times; from about two million pounds in 1784 to just short of six million in 1815. It fluctuated widely around the latter figure for most of the succeeding years to 1833. The point should first of all be made that when real costs, especially those of food or wheat, are taken into account, expenditure-patterns appear considerably less sensational, and the inexorably snow-balling effect partially disappears.[1] On the other hand, there were sharp increases within given periods, and these help to explain changes in social attitudes. Next, this entire period was one of massive population increases in town and country (albeit also one of great country–town migration), and if poor relief by years is given *per capita* of population, as Sir John Clapham did (see below), then the burden appears to be lessening during the twenties in given counties. Finally, much of the increase, especially before 1802, cannot be attributed to the effects of 'Speenhamland-type' relief as such; not only does the price inflation of the wartime years have to be taken into account, but every county of England and Wales shows an increase of roughly this order. As is shown in the official *Abstract of Returns Relative to the State of the Poor* (H.C. 175, 1804), those counties most affected by developing trade and industry, like Lancashire, Derbyshire, Notts., Stafford and the West Riding, were spending just as much on their poor, in the mid-eighties and 1802, as in what later became the Speenhamland counties; and what is more important, the proportionate money relief increases were comparable as between the two groups. Subsequently, however, the *per capita* relief figures of the industrialised counties look small indeed.

With such thoughts in mind, we are justified in asking whether the post-war burden of the Poor Law was such a heavy one as has often been assumed. In 1815–22, attitudes to the poor began to change – but were such changes in attitude justified by the facts? Sir John Clapham suggested that contemporary objectors to the Poor Law tended to exaggerate the nature of the burden which it imposed; 9s. or 10s. a year per head of population might appear 'a formidable figure

[1] Baugh, *op cit.*, pp. 56–60.

in the hands of anti-poor law statisticians', but there was
another and more balanced way of looking at the matter.
About 2s. a week 'was...the least on which (each individual
in) a family of four or five could subsist, at the absolute
minimum standard of comfort, during the 'twenties'. On that
scale, '9s. 9d. would have kept the whole population for
rather less than five weeks, or between 8 and 9 per cent of the
population, including an appropriate proportion of infants in
arms, for the whole year'.[1] A French witness before the
Commission of 1832, meanwhile, thought that relief expenditure of this order was a burden that England could easily
bear!

The burden had become seemingly fixed by that date, and
the anti-poor law Englishman could have retorted that it
showed no real signs of shrinking in those areas of the
country which were least able to bear it. There is now reason
to think, however, that the greatest pressures for change came
from farmers and landlords, who created the political atmosphere in which the critics and philosophers could articulate
their views. As Dr Digby has recently pointed out in a general
survey of the Poor Law in the nineteenth century, the value
of farming land, judged in terms of movements of rentals,
lagged well behind the poor rates which land-occupiers and
landlords had to pay. Hence, there was a rise of 62 per cent in
the money values of poor rates between 1802–3 and 1832–3,
but of only 25 per cent in the gross values of farm land.[2] It is
not clear whether farmers or landlords carried the major part
of the burden, but it is certain that there was some friction
between members of the same groups, and the farmers in a
parish were expected to pay poor rates. Great landlords, for
their part, had much influence over the policies of the nation,
and were calling for reliefs for their tenants, in, e.g. 1821–2.
The answer to Question 36 of the 'Answers to Rural Queries'
(1832) often stresses that farming capital was 'diminishing'.
However it must be stressed that the crucial opinion-forming
period lay within the nine or ten years following the end of

[1] J. H. Clapham, *An Economic History of Modern Britain*, vol. I (1950 edn.), pp. 362–4.
[2] Anne Digby, *The Poor Law in Nineteenth-Century England and Wales* (Historical Association pamph. General Series 104, 1982), p. 9.

the Napoleonic Wars, when a succession of good harvests (especially in 1820–22), tended to bring wheat prices to considerably less than half the wartime level (Table 1). At the same time, relief expenditure reached unprecedented heights during these years, and a high absolute burden (the peak years being 1817–19) was replaced by an even more galling drain in real terms in 1821–2, when the absolute levels of relief spending undoubtedly fell, but when prices fell even faster.[1] This undoubtedly bleak phase for landlords and farmers coincided with the publication of the Census of 1821, which indicated high rates of population increase in virtually all rural districts (Table 3). Malthus had in 1817 drawn attention to the social threat represented by the allowance system, and the census returns justified his arguments triumphantly – or so it must have appeared.

The hardening of opinion against the administration of the Poor Law, then, marked by the disorder of the post-war years and the Committee Reports on the Poor Laws of 1817 and 1818, undoubtedly reached an important stage in 1821–2; and it can be no accident that the Nottinghamshire 'reforms' began to attract publicity at this stage. The reforms were promulgated by Lowe, Becher and Nicholls, and aimed at a fundamental reorganisation of poor relief on much harsher lines, the central feature being a deterrent workhouse. Nicholls also explicitly attacked allowances: 'Is there a farmer throughout the Kingdom who has not a part of his labour ... performed at the expense of the parish?' (July, 1821). The answer was 'yes' – there were plenty in Nottinghamshire, which was very far from being a problem county, but Nicholls, whose reputation as a Poor Law administrator should not be allowed to obscure his mediocrity as a thinker and investigator, was on the point of teaching others how to rationalise their prejudices, and the winds of opinion were

[1] A discussion of the relationship of Poor Law expenditure and price movements, with special reference to harvests, is in M. Blaug, 'The Myth of the Old Poor Law and the Making of the New', *Journal of Economic History*, XXIII (1963), pp. 162–6, 180–1. As will be seen, some of Dr. Blaug's indices are reproduced in Table 1, and I have attempted to present the essence of his arguments while not doing violence to them. Dr. Daniel Baugh's paper (see note 1, p. 22) adds further detail.

blowing favourably for him. The latter soon afterwards blew gently, and, as the subjoined statistics show (Table 1), national relief expenditure did not grow appreciably, in absolute money values or real terms, for several years following 1822, and despite an upward movement in 1826–32, it never fully regained its post-war oppressiveness. But the upward trend of 1830–2, allied to rural unrest, is an important consideration in the story of the events which led to the Poor Law Commission.

There is certainly nothing in the official statistics of the period to prove that the Speenhamland-type burden was, after the early 'twenties, adding seriously to the national charge, and Blaug has shown (see his indices in Section 7 of Table 1) that the Speenhamland counties, as already designated, expended poor relief in year-by-year proportions which exhibit consistent sympathy with the relief figures for other groups of counties. However, *per capita* figures of annual relief in the Speenhamland counties are known to have been high, and it will also be in place to stress the additional observation that rural population growth rates in these counties are now known to have been low (Table 3) in the 'twenties and 'thirties. But this was a trend that could not have been known to the propagandists of the 'twenties, and the Poor Law Commission certainly did not draw this fact – apparently so destructive of its Malthusian hypothesis – to the public attention. Even before the third decade of the century, relief figures in the respective groups of counties moved in broad harmony, thereby, it might be thought, failing to indicate the working of an extraneous 'Speenhamland' factor in any one of those groups. Mere comparative expenditure figures cannot, however significant they may be in a broad sense, give us any idea of the dominant perceptions and social insecurities in large tracts of England. It is important to remember that major parts of the southern countryside were in ferment in 1816 and in 1830, and that sporadic rick-burning and breaking of threshing-machines took place between those years. That these violent reactions on the part of labourers arose from poverty and misery has never been doubted, and it is equally certain that local Poor Law administrators found much difficulty in dealing with them,

27

Table 1. *Expenditure on Poor Relief in England and Wales, 1812–32,*

	(1) Est. mid-year population[a]	(2) Total poor relief expenditure[b]	(3) Approx. expend. per head of population		(4) Wheat prices[c]	
	000's	£000's	s.	d.	s.	d.
1802	9,130	4,078	8	11	69	10
1812	10,480	6,676	12	9	126	6
1813	10,650	6,295	11	10	109	9
1814	10,820	5,419	10	0	74	4
1815	11,004	5,725	9	10	65	7
1816	11,196	6,911	12	4	78	6
1817	11,378	7,871	12	1	96	11
1818	11,555	7,517	13	0	86	3
1819	11,723	7,330	12	6	74	6
1820	11,903	6,959	11	8	67	10
1821	12,106	6,359	10	6	56	1
1822	12,320	5,773	9	5	44	7
1823	12,529	5,737	9	2	53	4
1824	12,721	5,787	9	1	63	11
1825	12,903	5,929	9	2	68	6
1826	13,074	6,441	9	10	58	8
1827	13,247	6,298	9	4	58	6
1828	13,438	6,332	9	5	60	5
1829	13,625	6,829	10	0	66	3
1830	13,805	6,799	9	10	64	3
1831	13,994	7,037	10	1	66	4
1832	14,165	6,791	9	7	58	8
1833	14,328	6,317	8	10	52	11

(a) See Mitchell and Deane, *Abstract of British Historical Statistics*, p. 8.

(b) For outline of sources, mainly in Sessional Papers, *op. cit.*, p. 410. Up to 1815, church and by-highway rates were probably included.

(c) For sources, Mitchell and Deane, *op. cit.*, p. 488.

(5) Index of relief in terms of wheat prices; and description of harvest[d] (1802 = 100)		(6) Gayer, Rostow and Schwartz, wholesale commod. index (domestic and imported)[e] (1821–5 = 100)		(7) Indices of poor relief expenditure in terms of county distributions (after Blaug)[f]			
				(i) Speenhamland counties	(ii) Other counties	(iii) Agricultural counties	(iv) Non-agricultural counties
100		122·2	(1802)	100	100	100	100
90	Poor	163·7	(1812)	170	161	169	160
98	Good	168·9	(1813)	145	160	152	155
125	Good	153·7	(1814)	125	139	128	137
149	Good	129·9	(1815)	130	150	136	143
151	Poor	118·6	(1816)	170	171	170	170
139	Poor	131·9	(1817)	190	197	193	193
148		138·7	(1818)	180	190	181	187
168		128·1	(1819)	172	185	171	185
176	Good	115·4	(1820)	163	176	164	175
194	Good	99·7	(1821)	150	160	153	158
223	Good	87·9	(1822)	143	140	140	142
185	Poor	97·6	(1823)	139	142	144	140
155	Poor	101·9	(1824)	140	143	146	140
148	Poor	113·0	(1825)	145	146	149	140
188		100·0	(1826)	151	162	153	161
184		99·3	(1827)	147	162	150	158
179	Poor	96·4	(1828)	150	160	154	155
170	Poor	95·8	(1829)	165	169	167	170
182	Poor	94·5	(1830)	163	169	167	170
182	Poor	95·3	(1831)	170	176	173	173
199	Good	91·5	(1832)	163	170	166	170
	Good	88·6	(1833)	146	169	153	155

(d) Blaug's calculations, *Journal of Economic History*, XXIII (1963), p. 180.

(e) Mitchell and Deane average of the monthly figures in Gayer, Rostow and Schwartz, *The Growth and Fluctuation of the British Economy*, vol. I, pp. 468–70.

(f) Blaug's figures, *Journal of Economic History*, vol. XXIII, pp. 180–1.

even when, as in 1830 in Kent and Sussex, the representations by poor labourers and their families were often peaceful. In some known instances, labourers are recorded as having demanded family allowances – 'is 9s. a week sufficient for a married man with a family?' (Sussex, 1830).[1] This type of campaigning took place frequently at a parish level, and the reaction of central government was to strengthen the hand of the property owner and the professional local administrator – examples being the Sturges Bourne Acts of 1818 and 1819, which provided for the drastic reorganisation of parish vestries.

Widespread concentration upon arable farming, with its large-scale seasonal labour demands in the summer and autumn, tended, in any case, to create a large reserve of labour which was not fully employed for more than half the year. It is instructive, as the present writer has done, to study the wage books of a large estate of this period, and to find only a dozen labourers employed in mid-winter, but the number of seasonally employed swelling the numbers at work on the estate to several times that number in the autumn. Some workers were women, who augmented the incomes of families, and even children; but the casual labour force was clearly large, nearly all the work being concerned with arable or cereal cultivation. Next, it is sometimes forgotten that already low wages were reduced, as (in some cases known to the writer) in 1818–20 and 1821–3, and it is clear that the poor man did not benefit from falling food and other prices for very long.

We are left with the thought, argued by others besides Dr. Blaug, that poor relief was a response to underemployment or 'disguised unemployment'. Unfortunately, empirical studies of regional and local price movements and labour conditions, as relating to this period and topic, are rare; but, for the time being, it appears likely that low incomes and precarious employment, general throughout rural districts of England and Wales, are much more important in their implications for

---

[1] Cf. A. Charlesworth, 'Radicalism, political crisis and the agricultural labourers' protests of 1830', in *Rural Social Change and Conflicts Since 1500* (Humberside College, 1982), esp. pp. 43–4; also J. Lowerson in the same volume, pp. 56–7.

patterns of poor relief, than are the precise modes of relief administration in themselves.[1] Areas which lacked alternative employments were more likely to suffer from endemically low agricultural wages, but it is important to remember that these areas experienced high losses from population migration.

Blaug's reference to the scaling of family allowances 'in accordance with the price of foodstuffs' will cause the student to seek some relationship between relief expenditures and wheat or other prices. Dr. Blaug produced considerable evidence to show that such expenditures bore some relationship to movements in wheat prices. Dr. Daniel Baugh has more recently taken this matter further, and has shown that the relationship of wheat prices and poor relief, whilst most certainly close, could vary somewhat from county to county, but also from period to period. Hence, from 1793 to 1814, poor relief in seriously affected southern counties like Kent, Essex and Sussex was evidently a response to high food prices rather than to unemployment, the point being that the wartime years displayed a heavy demand for rural labour, even though 'seasonal unemployment could never be completely eliminated'.[2]

Professor McCloskey has shown that given such a constant demand for labour, any attempt to lower wages by farmers – in the knowledge that the parish would add any necessary subsistence through poor relief – would be unlikely to have any lasting economic effect. Wage subsidies were assumed to reduce effort on the part of the labourer; but, as McCloskey argues, any major lessening of the supply of labour would have caused wages to rise, given a stable demand curve for that labour. Higher wages would, in turn, result in lower poor relief expenditures.[3]

Such calculations suggest yet another reason for supposing that the variants of 'Speenhamland' relief arrangements were

[1] Blaug, 'The Myth of the Old Poor Law and the Making of the New', *Journal of Economic History*, XIII (1963) pp. 167–70.

[2] Baugh, *op cit.*, 59.

[3] Donald N. McCloskey, 'New Perspectives on the Old Poor Law', *Explorations in Economic History*, X (1973), p. 427.

not only negligible in their total effects, but were mere reactions to more general economic circumstances, and that total poor relief expenditure movements throughout England and Wales reflected those circumstances. Following 1820, the demand for rural labour was much less intense, and a greater degree of agricultural unemployment undoubtedly swelled relief bills. But there is no reason whatever to suppose that village populations remained non-migratory and static during the twenties, in the south and elsewhere.

How was the 'Pauper Host' Constituted?

TO Nicholls and his colleagues, the pauper was a potential Jacobin, lurking in incalculable numbers beyond every corner and making ready to 'prey on the property of ... richer neighbours'. Paupers were fairly numerous in Southwell, if we are to believe this earnest reformer, and the *Abstract of Returns Relative to the Relief of the Poor for 1812–15* reveals that there were in the town, in 1815, 120 adult poor persons permanently, and 76 occasionally relieved. But the population of this country town was 2674 in 1821, and the 'host' (which does not include children) was therefore well removed in relative magnitude from the pauper proportion of 12 or 13 per cent of total national population estimated for the period of the returns mentioned. Probably this national proportion increased, at least temporarily, during the crisis years of 1818 and 1819, although the possibility suggested by Professor Krause that 'over 20 per cent of the population was on relief between 1817 and 1821'[1] looks slightly less terrifying if the total indicated is broken down in terms of age, sex, fitness to work and duration of relief. Unfortunately, the official returns do not enable us to do this with any accuracy for the years mentioned by Krause, and his own suggestion is in any

[1] J. T. Krause, 'Changes in English Fertility and Mortality, 1781–1850', *Economic History Review*, XI (1958), p. 66. But for more recent work on this period, *vide* G. S. L. Tucker, 'The Old Poor Law Revisited', *Explorations in Economic History*, XII (1975).

case based upon conjecture. The only comparatively detailed breakdowns of pauper classifications obtainable are those in the similar *Abstract of Returns* for 1802–3 (H.C. 175), and, while these are not statistically complete (they give separate totals for adults and children outside, but not *inside*, local poorhouses and they probably embody the results of extensive double-counting), the available categories do enable some useful calculations to be made. The primary aim of any calculation must be that of ascertaining roughly how many members of the 'host' were able-bodied males, for the significant controversies, and their relationship to reality, devolved largely on the size of this social element.

It can of course be objected that the figures for 1802–3 (the official returns then related to a period running from each Easter to that in the year following), can bear little relationship to those of the crisis years nearly two decades later. This is certainly a possibility that has to be taken into account, and any deductions from the pauper totals for the respective years have to allow not only for the inadequacies of the classification themselves, but also for the general inaccuracies of the statistics, in so far as they relate to the whole of this period before 1835. As the Webbs warned, 'the returns represented, not the numbers simultaneously on relief on any one day, but the total numbers of different persons ... repeatedly applying for relief during a part ... of the year'.[1] The 1812–15 totals relate to adults only. However, a comparison of presumed successful applications for relief, on the part of adult paupers in 1802–3 and 1812–15, is still a useful operation, even in the largely negative sense that it provides a warning against reading too much into pauper totals on the one hand or figures for annual expenditure on the other. We are reminded that there was no fixed relationship between the amounts spent on paupers and their numbers in a given period and district, and even the rough calculations of sums spent *per capita*, nationally and at the county level (Tables 1 and 3), could conceal increases or decreases in the numbers of persons actually relieved. However, and as will be seen, there is somewhat more reassurance in the figures than this would

[1] Webb, *op cit.*, p. 1039.

imply, and in the cases of a number of the most important Speenhamland counties, the totals of successful applications for relief (and existing book entries) show quite credible common tendencies:

Adults on permanent relief out of the poorhouse

	1802–3	1812–13	1813–14	1814–15	County population, 000s	
					1801	1811
Sussex	9,415	14,472	14,099	13,058	159	190
Berks.	5,620	9,453	9,074	7,175	111	120
Wilts.	12,500	16,009	15,144	13,355	184	192
Oxford	6,539	7,792	7,635	7,134	112	120

Wheat prices per quarter: (1802) 69s. 10d.; (1812) 126s. 6d.; (1813) 109s. 9d.; (1814) 74s. 4d.

The figures, for what they are worth, indicate that adult permanent pauperism increased considerably faster than population in these 'problem' counties, but also that the numbers of relief cases could fluctuate in a downward direction. The above particulars suggest that economies were being introduced by parishes. It should be added that the 'occasionally' relieved categories, for the same counties, show similar tendencies, and for this reason alone it would be most unwise to dismiss the figures as meaningless. Handled carefully, they afford suggestive insights if none of the precision that modern statisticians demand. They serve to remind us that the composition of the pauper population may have changed from time to time, and also that, in a number of the most serious cases, there was a burden of pauper numbers out of all proportion to any presumed local development in population, agriculture and industry. This being said, the returns do not allow accurate calculations of pauper percentages in relation to county and national totals, and any attempted calculation is likely to give an exaggerated result in consequence of the double-counting referred to. The Webbs, using a fixed sum of £6 a year in individual relief payment as the basis of their calculations, suggested that during this period the percentage of all kinds of pauperism in England and Wales rose from 8.6 per cent (1803) to 12.7 per cent (1813), and then to 13.2 per cent in 1818.

The relatively little-used *Abstract of Returns* for 1802–3 provides valuable figures which have already awakened critical discussion. The latter turns on definitions of an able-bodied person, or pauper. If Williams and the present writer disagree on this subject, then it can only be said that the differing views were shared by parish overseers in 1828, according to a parliamentary return of that year.[1] At Salehurst in Sussex, 1096 persons were relieved out of a total of 2121 inhabitants, but only 120 were seen as able-bodied. At Brade, all the 108 persons relieved were 'able-bodied', but at Ashurst, only 30 out of 282 cases were thus classified; and at Ewhurst, only 63 out of 520. A sample of 17 Sussex, Buckinghamshire and Westmorland sets of parish statistics indicates that between 20 and 30 per cent of relief cases were seen as able-bodied. Sometimes children – in an able-bodied pauper's family – were included in the statistics, and sometimes they were not.

To see all such children as belonging to the able-bodied category, whether for economic or social purposes, is plainly unsatisfactory, if not nonsensical. Indeed, pauper adults may often have been so because of persistent ill-health. But, leaving this aside, Williams suggests that there were roughly 600,000 'able-bodied men and their dependants on relief through the year 1802–3', and assumes that 'the typical able-bodied family consisted of man, wife and four children'. In point of fact, if we include those persons relieved occasionally, the figures for 1802–3 produce no more than two children per likely couple[2] or a possibly high number of single adults, who were, of course, more footloose by definition. *Some* of the children may have been Mark Blaug's third or fourth in given families.

[1] *Parl. Papers*, 1829, xxi, esp. pp. 95–7. ('Abstract of the Number of Poor Persons belonging to several Parishes … between 25 March 1827 and 25 March 1828'; this return concentrates on able-bodied paupers.)
[2] *Vide* Williams, *op cit.*, pp. 42–4; cf. also his valuable Table 4.2, p. 150, which produces a variant of the data given on Table 2 overleaf (p. 34 *infra*).

Table 2. Approximate pauper classifications in supposed Speenhamland-type counties, based on book entries and relief cases for the period, Easter 1802–Easter 1803

County	(1) No. of rural parishes	(2) Total 1801 population (000)	(3) Total pauper cases, all types (000)	(4) Pauper percentage of population	(6) Propn. of elderly and infirm of all paupers %	(5) Per capita expenditure s. d.	(7) Persons on permanent out-relief (i) Total (000)	(7) Persons on permanent out-relief (ii) Total of children under 15 (000)	(7) Persons on permanent out-relief (iii) Total of percentage of children
Sussex	313	159	37·0	23	9	22 6	26·4	16·9	72
Wilts.	374	184	42·1	23	12	13 11	29·4	16·9	57
Berks.	222	111	22·6	20	13	15 1	12·8	7·5	58
Bucks.	230	108	19·6	18	13	16 1	13·0	6·5	50
Dorset	305	114	15·9	14	20	11 4	10·4	4·6	45
Hunts.	107	38	4·7	13	13	12 2	3·1	1·5	48
Suffolk	525	214	36·1	13	12	11 5	16·2	8·1	50
Bedford	141	63	7·3	12	16	11 9	4·5	2·0	44
England and Wales (all parts)	15,535	9,235	1,041	11	16	8 11	551·3	315·1	61

Note: children 'in any house of industry or workhouse' were not separately distinguished, nor were those of persons 'occasionally' relieved.

It is certainly the case that the most notorious of the later 'Speenhamland' counties showed itself to have a worse than average pauper problem by that year. Several of these were apparently 'problem' counties in the period 1785–1802, and, once more, it seems unrealistic to look for the sources of their troubles in administrative methods alone. To this extent, we are surely justified in laying special emphasis on the winter unemployment in increasingly arable areas, and on the low wages – relative to high prices – to which bread scales were a reaction at a later stage. What we are seeing, however, is the provision of relief, often for short periods, to people in desperate need, and the precise method, given too much attention, can be simply seen as a red herring. D. A. Baugh's calculations for 'Speenhamland' and 'non-Speenhamland' parishes in Essex, Kent and Sussex show remarkably similar trends, and in the case of Essex and Sussex, similar levels in poor relief spending from 1800 to 1834. Dr. Baugh suggests that, on balance, family allowances were a post-war or even a twenties' phenomenon in these high-spending counties.[1] This, of course, is in contradiction to Mark Blaug's thesis that many parishes were abandoning allowances, although it is certainly the case that scattered parishes did so. For the rest, even the 1802–3 statistics do not tell us how many recipients of relief were really 'able-bodied' in the literal, as distinct from Williams's rather pedantic sense.

As we have seen, there could be great disagreement about 'able-bodiedness' even in given or selected parishes a few years before 1834, and there can be little doubt that the Poor Law Commission, and many of those who performed propaganda exercises before its deliberations took place, exaggerated the nature of the problem. Fortunately, case studies, whether merely empirical or not, are now beginning to expose the inconsistencies between the anti-pauper ideologies of the time, and the richly varied situations within individual parishes and regions. Nor is the individual parish irrelevant, and it is well to examine the immediate circumstances which conditioned its outlook.

Agitation against the Old Poor Law was often based on purely parochial experience – the Nottinghamshire experi-

[1] Baugh, op cit., pp. 63–7.

ments and attitudes provide some illustrative examples – and it is the parish as a microcosm that we must consider. English rural society, from the mid-eighteenth century, was being struck by unemployment and underemployment new in quality and quantity. The latter had none of the anonymity which is associated with more recent mass industrial unemployment, for it was being experienced in a small face-to-face community which felt the financial burden just as keenly as it recognised the human problem, and which was likely to react more extremely in its attitudes and measures than the larger urban society which was evolving.[1] It can reasonably be argued that the Justices who met at Speenhamland, and the local officers who gave information to the Assistant Commissioners over a generation later, were in fact transmitting common opinion at the level of intense but blinkered local feeling, and in a situation where the condition of the helpless, the surliness of the potential rioter, and the studied carelessness of the occasional subsidised labourer were immediately magnified together or in turn. Nor is this tendency to magnification, or to sensitive reaction, to be accounted an ineluctable weakness, for under the Old Poor Law varied problems were fairly sensibly recognised and dealt with, however short-sightedly. The old system had both humanity and flexibility.

Reaction to the problems, however, was inevitably influenced by the size of the farmer's and ratepayer's purse. The average parish, in one of the Speenhamland counties listed, consisted of rather over 600 persons, of whom (at the worst periods of unemployment) one-seventh to one-fifth were in receipt of some kind of relief, permanent or occasional. The total annual bill for that relief would be about £500 in the most common cases, falling on forty or fifty main ratepayers, who had other rates and taxes to pay in addition. The

[1] It should be mentioned that Dr. Blaug, after careful examination of the problem, rejects the thesis that poor-relief payments were higher in small parishes. But that argument is not pursued here. Mark Neuman (cf. the other points made on this page) suggests that high poor-relief bills can be attributed to the desire of frequently non-resident magistrates to create a charitable image; cf. his essay, 'Speenhamland in Berkshire' in Martin (ed.), *Comparative Development in Social Welfare*, pp. 116–18.

response of these ratepayers, whose reaction to the notion of higher wages as a solution is perfectly explicable in these circumstances, was to seek to make use of labour when summer employment justified that use, and to keep families alive during the rest of the year. However, as we have seen, the number of ostensibly able-bodied labourer paupers could vary greatly in each parish, and actual examples show that in 1827–8 the numbers involved could present formidable totals on paper. Close examination reveals curiosities: Brade in Sussex, with a population of 903, had 108 able-bodied males in receipt of relief 'with their families', but we learn that 33 were 'on highways', and 75 'occasional'. Shipley, with a population of 1159, had 133 able-bodied men relieved, but 46 received 'allowances for children', 40 had cottage rents paid, and 47 were on highway work. The percentage totals of all paupers, in terms of the entire local populations, moved roughly round the proportions suggested, but it is very clear that those relieved were not all permanent recipients of parish assistance, or that they received small sums (cottage rents were about £5 a year).

The fact remains that in all but the worst parishes, the majority of labouring families were *not*, at most periods, consistently in receipt of any relief, and it must remain a matter for wonderment how they survived effectively at all. If their pauper brethren were demoralised, their own morale must have been correspondingly high. Meanwhile, there are grounds for supposing that the pauper problem at the Speenhamland parish and other levels was much more complex than common accounts suggest, for illegitimacy – a growing factor at this period, the tendency of low nutrition to produce early ageing and sickness, the slow destruction of local crafts and alternative employments, the conservatism of all but very young labourers, and the existence of kinship bonds and limited mutual assistance among some families,[1] would in any case tend to encourage a growing but varied pauper group. This group would in turn tend to have a stable core little affected by any given form of relief. To attribute the growth of the group primarily to reckless fecundity,

[1] As an influence discouraging migration.

encouraged by bread scales on the part of one section of it, is (in the absence of firm evidence) a most serious historical *non sequitur*.

There are signs (e.g. from parishes in Bucks.) that wage subsidies were most certainly practised, as at Great Horwood and Whaddon, among a very large section of the labouring population, and the search for 'Speenhamland' practices is by no means worthless. But these are usually taken to mean family allowances, especially by disciples of Malthus, and little real testing of the likely effects of the latter forms of relief had been performed until Dr. James P. Huzel[1] began to subject parishes to examination in the 1960s.

Pauperism and Population Pressures

SINCE this booklet was reprinted in 1979, Dr. James P. Huzel has thrown further light on the probable soundness of Malthusian views of the demographic effect of allowances, and has greatly expanded the area of his research to take in 22 parishes in 15 counties, as well as 49 parishes within the county of Kent. The object of the research was that of testing the Malthusian hypothesis, and that of the Poor Law Commissioners of 1834, 'that parish allowances, in addition to facilitating population growth, also rooted the labourer to his parish of settlement, thus restricting labour mobility'.[2]

As has been pointed out, the publication of the 1821 census returns would almost certainly have confirmed them in this belief, given, of course, that family allowances were well rooted in most parishes. These returns show that the inter-censal rural population increases[3] (1811–21) for at least five of

[1] James P. Huzel, 'Malthus, the Poor Law and Population', *Economic History Review*, 2nd ser., XXII (1969), pp. 430–52.
[2] James P. Huzel, 'The Demographic Impact of the Old Poor Law; More Reflections on Malthus', *Economic History Review*, XXXIII, No. 3, Aug. 1980, pp. 367–81.
[3] For these rural increases (see also Table 3), *vide* R. Price Williams, *Journal of the R. Statistical Soc.*, XLIII, 1880, pp. 482–3.

the so-called 'Speenhamland' counties were above the national average for such rural districts, and most of the other counties in this category – except, surprisingly, Berkshire and Wiltshire – exhibited rural rates fairly close to this very high average. But the difference between 'Speenhamland' and 'non-Speenhamland' areas, in so far as it is possible to distinguish them clearly, was not great. The evidence for such influence or direct association (with allowances) is certainly not of a kind that would satisfy the modern social demographer, who would inevitably ask what parishes and specific districts had reached a critical point in their use of these relief methods, and what were the birth and fertility-rates in those localities in the years in which the methods were fully utilised – or in which they were absent.

Dr. Huzel has in fact done this, using even more demographic variables for the three decades 1801–30, and he has gone to immense trouble in identifying which Kent parishes used given forms of allowance, and which did not. Before discussing, briefly, the refinements in his analyses, it should be mentioned that his findings tend to rebut Mark Blaug's argument that child allowances were, in effect, a welfare mechanism that saved the lives of young children. Huzel has even experimented with the measurable effects of allowances in Kent parishes where these affected the first, third or fourth child in a family – in the sense that they were given only on the arrival of such a child – and there is no real evidence that poor persons were rushed into improvident marriages by such payments,[1] even where they appeared to offer temptation to produce a first child.

Huzel's findings on migration-rates from parishes for decades (for each 1000 of population *per annum*) are no less interesting, and all parishes utilising allowance scales reveal net losses by migration, i.e. in Kent samples, for the 1820s. The Malthusian hypothesis hardly held good here, and labour mobility was not severely hindered, by all appearances. Similar questions are raised by an examination of the generally low rural population growth rates for the 1820s, which held for 'Speenhamland' as for other counties. Deane and

[1] Huzel, *op cit.*, pp. 379–80.

Cole have indicated the relationships of the absolute population increases and natural increases of, and estimated migration figures to and from English counties between 1801 and 1831. It is instructive to find that one of the leading Speenhamland counties, Wiltshire, had a high rate of estimated natural increase but very heavy apparent loss by emigration to other areas, and that Berkshire seems to have had a very similar history.[1] Of other Speenhamland counties, Buckingham, Dorset, Huntingdon and Oxford apparently lost through such migration one-quarter to one-third of their total natural increase for the three decades, while on the other hand Sussex and Bedfordshire had comparatively small losses through such outward migration. In other words, the very imperfect data available (which rest chiefly on the unsatisfactory Rickman parish register abstracts) show no recognisably significant common tendency, but do suggest that movements of people even from supposedly pauperised or stagnating agricultural areas could be much greater than contemporary propagandists against the Old Poor Law would have had us believe. The aggregated data, for counties, given in Table 3, contain another item of interest; they give *per capita* figures for poor relief based on rural populations, and where country areas – as here given – experienced relatively slow rates of population growth following 1821, then the expenditure figures would appear to be inflated when compared with those of an industrialising county like Nottinghamshire. The high rates of rural population growth in the latter county will be noted, and resembled those of Lancashire.

Even where there was higher-than-average expenditure on the poor in samples from 344 Kent parishes examined by Huzel, then there was *greater* out-migration from those relatively pauperism-affected parishes in which more relief was given. A little imaginative insight will show why this was so; a single and footloose labourer would try his luck elsewhere, and paupers, like all other categories of human being, cannot simply be viewed as constituting one insensate lump. Kent, of course, was one of those counties affected by the massive influence of the metropolis. Hence, we have two

[1] P. Deane and W. A. Cole, *British Economic Growth 1688–1959* (1964), pp. 108–9.

possible factors at work; a turnover of population which has long been known to historical demographers as obtaining in the remotest parishes, and the tendency of high expenditure figures to appear where there was relative loss of people in rural areas.

The present writer has been at pains to point out that the stimuli to migration could be manifold, and that they could embody positive (i.e. attractive) as well as negative (or propulsive) forms.[1] Blaug draws attention to county wage-levels[2] and to their tendency to rise near London, but it is certain that higher wages were only one of a dozen considerations that moved the countryman onward from his parish. Employment for women and children, and the failures of that employment, were at least as important, and the idea of scaled allowances as a dominant factor amidst so many other factors can assume disproportionate importance.

Meanwhile, Huzel has shown that allowances were not given in any immediately simple form; some Kent parishes gave 'allowances in aid of wages' combined with child allowances by scale, some the first but not the second, some gave child allowances only, and some gave neither allowances in aid of wages nor child allowances. There has been some discussion of the relative importance of wage subsidies and income supplements, but it is now fairly clear that neither had much significance for fertility or for population movements.

The most telling empirical refutation of the notion of a rural population tied to its parishes by poor relief lies not so much in demographic calculations, which can conceal complex processes, but in the very speed at which towns grew throughout England before 1832. Even in the case of southern towns, growth rates in excess of 20 per cent per decade were not at all uncommon, and much of this growth was made possible by in-migration from southern regions. The stereotype of a highly mobile Midlands and north-west, and a stagnating south, surely awaits the most serious critical examination.

[1] Marshall, 'The Lancashire Rural Labourer in the Early Nineteenth Century', *Trans. of the Lancashire and Cheshire Antiquarian Society*, LXXI, 1961, pp. 94–5.
[2] 'The Myth of the Old Poor Law', p. 170.

Table 3. Rates of rural population increase in counties deemed to have

Group 1 – counties with low or falling rates of rural population increase,
of child allowances in 1832.

Group 2 – counties with above average rates of rural population increase,
of child allowances in 1832.

Group 3 – counties with above average rates of rural population increase,
(S) = designated as Speenhamland county, *Select Committee*

	Intercensal population increases, rural districts including small towns of less than 2000 inhabitants			
	1801–11 %	1811–21 %	1821–31 %	1831–41 %
Group 1				
Sussex (S)	13·61	14·70	7·13	7·33
Bucks. (S)	7·29	14·83	7·57	7·12
Wilts. (S)	4·23	11·28	7·71	6·42
Berks. (S)	7·35	9·80	7·86	8·21
Suffolk (S)	8·61	15·13	8·07	4·60
Oxford (S)	6·75	13·17	9·29	1·24
Devon (S)	10·01	13·78	8·59	5·38
Essex (S)	10·63	14·55	8·32	7·97
Northants. (S)	6·43	14·17	7·07	7·71
Group 2				
Huntingdon (S)	10·54	16·71	6·71	10·64
Cambs. (S)	13·73	19·75	12·51	13·89
Somerset	10·52	16·66	14·14	7·59
Group 3				
Notts. (S)	16·34	13·47	19·54	14·20
Lincoln	11·79	18·38	10·96	13·20
Indeterminate				
Warwick (S)	3·52	15·11	4·46	11·24
Leicester (S)	11·54	12·00	5·60	6·23
Average increases, rural districts of England and Wales	12·11	14·72	10·52	9·69
Average, all areas England and Wales	14·30	18·06	15·81	14·48

and in which more than 50 per cent of sample parishes reported the use

and in which more than 50 per cent of sample parishes reported the use

and in which few reporting parishes used child allowances in 1832.
Agricultural Labourers, 1824.

| Average *per capita* relief expenditure on the poor | | | | Percentages of sample parishes reporting, 1832 | | | | |
| 1802 | 1812 | 1821 | 1831 | Giving allowances in aid of wages | Giving child allowances | Using bread scales | Using roundsman systems | Using labour rate |
s. d.	s. d.	s. d.	s. d.					
22 7	33 1	23 8	19 4	6	82	22	4	14
16 1	22 9	19 1	8 7	17	71	9	11	17
13 11	24 5	15 8	16 9	35	72	55	14	14
15 1	27 1	17 0	15 9	3	73	63	13	27
11 5	19 4	17 0	18 4	10	74	34	0	14
16 2	24 10	19 1	16 11	11	67	17	22	33
7 3	11 5	10 8	9 0	8	67	0	4	17
12 1	24 7	20 0	17 2	8	66	44	0	12
14 5	19 11	19 2	16 10	11	67	17	22	33
12 2	16 9	16 0	15 3	8	54	54	0	15
12 1	17 0	14 9	13 8	7	51	37	5	23
8 11	12 3	9 11	8 10	16	64	24	4	8
6 4	10 10	9 5	6 6	4	4	0	11	29
9 2	10 10	12 3	11 0	5	20	0	5	10
11 3	13 4	12 0	9 7	11	60	13	24	13
12 4	14 8	16 0	11 7	17	33	0	11	0
8 11	12 9	10 6	10 1	—	—	—	—	—

The Old Poor Law Reconsidered

WHAT, then, remains of the concepts made famous by the 1832 Commission? It should be stressed that it is far too early to assume that the Commissioners were always and everywhere wrong in their criticisms of the old system. The complex social fabric of England and Wales at that period would make any such assumption most undesirable. Moreover, an unsound hypothesis can still produce fruitful or factually valuable results, and the 1832 survey was a remarkable achievement of its kind. As Dr. Blaug's researches show, the potentialities of the Commission's material are very great, and the latter still has considerable uses to the economic, social and local historian. Nor should we make the mistake of unduly blaming the leading personalities of the Poor Law Commission for attitudes which were widespread at that time, and which, in somewhat transmuted form, have marked social and class relationships ever since. The supposedly idle and shiftless pauper of 1832, multiplying social burdens in immobility and vice, has his modern counterpart – in the minds of many – in the Pakistani immigrant allegedly living on Public Assistance and British welfare services. It is still more unhistorical to blame the Commissioners for not using modern survey techniques and the precautions associated with those techniques. It is the historian's task to trace the evolution of their ideas, irrespective of the relationships of the latter to social reality, and it is now fairly evident that the attitudes which ensured the acceptance of those ideas were already crystallising half a generation earlier – in the somewhat different circumstances of the immediate post-war years. Their hypothesis (relative to able-bodied idleness, 'predial slavery' and economic waste) was born in those years, and was applied when the economic situation of the country at large was rapidly changing. Lacking the data to look forward with hope, and therefore with humanity, the Commissioners looked backward and condemned. It was not in fact difficult to make a convincing-seeming case which appealed to ratepayers, landowners and many middle-class savants. The phrase 'Act of Elizabeth', representing antiquity and irrelevance, became more and more pejorative.

It is true to say that these attitudes were reproduced by many writers of history until about two decades ago, when Mark Blaug placed what was little less than a heavy charge of explosive under some complacent assumptions about the Old Poor Law, which, as he claimed, could produce 'a welfare state in miniature' in given parish conditions. Now, it is not difficult to go through parish overseers' and other records *in extenso*, and to show that sick persons really were cared for (*as far as certain entries permit us to conclude*), and that action on behalf of the destitute was based on at least some intimate knowledge of those persons relieved. Arrangements for mid-wifery were, in some cases, made by the parish authorities, and the medical services later provided under the post-1834 Poor Law were not without their antecedents. Although workhouse administration could pass through bewildering phases, some socially mixed vestries had the effect of prevent-ing farmers from misusing the roundsman system in their own interests.[1] On the other hand, many farmers had their excuses for extreme parsimony in the post-war years, and the pauper was hardly indulged; he or she was simply kept alive, but in conditions of more elaborate human contact than would have been feasible in a centralised Poor Law Union.

An exacting critic like Williams dismisses much of this work simply as one or other outline of a 'cultural configura-tion' of a local institution in operation, without demonstrable wider significance, and it is true that regional studies of the kind performed by Baugh, Huzel, Neuman and others carry far more weight in indicating what conditions *may* have been like over tracts of rural England. Williams, however, remarks that 'local and regional differences can only be rendered intelligible in a national context',[2] which is true enough provided that the national context is not seen to change shape as wide regions are discussed and examined – or is at least not

[1] Some dissertations on themes like this are now available, and an interesting work in the *genre* is the study of Hungerford in Berks., D. Stafford, 'A Gilbert Act Parish: the Relief and Treatment of the Poor in the Town and Parish of Hungerford, Berks., 1783–1834' (M.Phil. thesis, Univ. of Reading, 1983).
[2] Williams, *op cit.*, p. 35.

seen to be based on assumptions that render the broader view of national policy misleading. In certain areas of public administration, the regions and the centre are always to be seen as complementary.

The same lively critic dismisses much of the Poor Law historiography of the last twenty years as based on outmoded assumptions and on a limited stock of ideas. This somewhat unkind dismissal might be levelled at the modest local historian who bases his ideas on W. E. Tate's *The Parish Chest*; interestingly, however, it is the ingenious empirical testing of that period, set into train by Mark Blaug's challenges, that has brought the subject to life. For the rest, much of Williams's contribution is only indirectly concerned with establishing new truths about the Poor Law, but is instead concerned with much wider questions of historical methodology, and with the limitations of empirical investigation. Williams raises broad issues, but it should be made plain that most serious historians are well aware of the problems surrounding the form and reliability of historical evidence, whether the latter is projected into statistics or not. Such evidence cannot be equated with that commonly obtained by the natural scientist working in the controlled environment of the laboratory. There can be little doubt that some, at least, of Williams's criticisms and warnings are timely, and his argumentation only becomes intriguing when he suggests that theorists like Malthus not only put forth views which were so set out as to be immune to testing, but which *are*, on that account, thus immune.[1] In fact, Malthus's later followers have tried to justify his theories by using received historical methods, and can be refuted in the same terms. Likewise, it has only recently become a major interest of Poor Law historians to question the findings of the Poor Law Commission. Twenty years is not long in historiographical terms.

It is not the purpose of this booklet to examine the working of the Poor Law Unions which followed the Poor Law Amendment Act of 1834, although it is in place to mention that the 'welfare' view of the Old Poor Law evidently struck deep roots in industrial Lancashire. In other words, accord-

[1] Williams, *op cit.*, p. 55.

ing to Dr. Midwinter and others,[1] the old system, as practised there, did not really need reform, because it was flexible and convenient, and the much higher level of industrial development of Lancashire made it easier to bear the costs of poor relief. The industrial employer was himself responsible for dismissing 'hands', even though he may have felt himself to be in the grip of forces beyond his control, and he had no interest in driving a reserve of unemployed workers beyond his parish and locality. These considerations are mentioned because it may too easily be assumed that the Old Poor Law was somehow ineluctably related to the backward, stagnating southern parish, awaiting only the hand of a Chadwick or a Senior to tear it away from an intolerable situation. The ideologists of Poor Law Reform expressed fears that the evils of the old system were developing in the industrial areas, but that was not how local and social leaders in those areas viewed the matter. Some Lancashire Poor Law Unions remained without a new-type workhouse for more than two decades.

The Poor Law Amendment Act is associated with the achievement of immediate and visible economies, and a rapid fall in the cost of relief throughout most areas of the country. While an account of its effects belongs to a separate and specialised study, there can be little doubt that at least some of the evils it was designed to destroy – social, economic and demographic – were in fact exaggerated. The 'true' Speenhamland system of wage subvention may well have been a minor factor by 1832; it is unlikely that the child allowances which were confused with this system had much demographic effect; and the economic problems which underlay the high relief bills of the Speenhamland counties were not of a kind which could have been removed by Senior and Chadwick. Wages remained low in those counties long after 1834, and it is doubtful whether the near-brutal economies practised by some of the new Guardians did much to alleviate their more general economic problems. On the other hand, the new Act is rightly regarded as having heralded an administrative revolution, and in so far as it led to the

[1] E. C. Midwinter, *Social Administration in Lancashire, 1830–1860* (Manchester, 1969), p. 14.

effective establishment of a new principle in the relationship of local and central government, perhaps it did something to curb, ultimately, those 'wild men' of *laissez faire* (and there were some in Lancashire) whose notion of local administration was that it should be so unobtrusive as to be virtually non-existent. The new organisation helped to limit the power of the rural tyrant, and it may have purged from the community a number of undesirable elements among recipients of relief and among part-time administrators. But while bureaucratic history must always have its fascinations, centralisation, boldness, professionalism and even ultimate effect are not the only criteria by which administrative reforms can be judged. Flexibility and sensitivity to human need, adjustment to local circumstances, comprehensiveness and local participation, are additional criteria of equal importance. We can learn quite as much from the Old Poor Law as from the New.

Select Bibliography

The major sources of information are still the Webbs' massive volumes carrying the general title *English Poor Law History* (vols VII, VIII and IX of their *English Local Government* (London, 1929). Since their material is apt to be intractable for many purposes of teaching and discussion, general surveys like Mr G. W. Oxley's study (below) can be invaluable. Otherwise, this booklet, and its bibliography, are obliged to concentrate on those contributions to discussion which seem most fundamental to an understanding of the subject. The studies by Poynter, Oxley and Williams (see below) contain excellent bibliographies.

D. A. Baugh, 'The Cost of Poor Relief in South East England, 1790–1834', *Economic History Review*, 28 (Feb. 1975), 50–68.

M. Blaug, 'The Myth of the Old Poor Law and the Making of the New', *Journal of Economic History*, 23, No. 2 (June 1963), 151–84.

M. Blaug, 'The Poor Law Report Re-examined', *Journal of Economic History*, 24 (June 1964), 229–45.

Both of the above are seminal studies. They have been heavily criticised, but have opened up discussion in a novel and fruitful way. They should be read for their many interesting ideas.

J. P. Huzel, 'Malthus, the Poor Law and Population in early nineteenth-century England', *Economic History Review*, 2nd Ser., 22 (Dec. 1969), 430–52.

J. P. Huzel, 'The Demographic Impact of the Old Poor Law: More Reflexions on Malthus', *Economic History Review*, 2nd Ser., 33 (Aug. 1980), 367–81.

These articles embody a considered and highly organised attack on the Malthusian position, and the second article is far-reaching in its examples. They are essential reading, as are Baugh's comments, for regional historians concerned with social change.

D. N. McCloskey, 'New Perspectives on the Old Poor Law', *Explorations in Economic History*, 10, No. 4 (1974), 419–36. An exploration of the likely impact of pauper labour supply on wage levels, using received economic analysis to expose a contradiction. It is theoretical only.

M. Neuman, 'Speenhamland in Berkshire', in E. W. Martin (ed.), *Comparative Development in Social Welfare* (London, 1972), pp. 85–127.

G. W. Oxley, *Poor Relief in England and Wales, 1601–1834* (Newton Abbot and London, 1974). A useful handbook with plenty of source material and interesting speculations.

J. R. Poynter, *Society and Pauperism: English Ideas on Poor Relief, 1795–1834* (London, 1969). An elegant study of the ideological background of the age.

G. S. L. Tucker, 'The Old Poor Law Revisited', *Explorations in Economic History*, 12, No. 3 (1975). This surveys fertility ratios by counties in 1821, and relates them to *per capita* poor relief expenditures, 1817–21.

J. S. Taylor, 'The Mythology of the Old Poor Law', *Journal of Economic History*, 29 (1969), 292–7. This is sharply critical of some of Dr. Blaug's assumptions, but is mainly interesting on technicalities.

Karel Williams, *From Pauperism to Poverty* (London, 1981). Contains a fine set of mainly parliamentary statistics, and lively attacks on almost anybody who has dared to write recently on the subject of this booklet. Contentious, complex, written in difficult prose, but worth much close attention.

Additional Reading

The following works will also be found illuminating, but often in a more general sense.

J. J. and A. J. Bagley, *The English Poor Law* (London, 1966), is a very useful general introduction to the subject.

T. C. Barker and J. R. Harris, *A Merseyside Town in the Industrial Revolution*, St. Helens, 1750–1900 (Liverpool, 1954). This has some useful material on the local treatment of the poor.

C. M. L. Bouch and G. P. Jones, *A Short Economic and Social History of the Lake Counties, 1500–1830* (Manchester, 1960), contains interesting sidelights on northern poor law administration and charities.

R. Boyson, 'The New Poor Law in North-East Lancashire, 1834–71', *Transactions of the Lancashire and Cheshire Antiquarian Society*, LXX (1960), shows how pre-1834 ideas lasted into the succeeding period of the New Poor Law.

A. W. Coats, 'Changing Attitudes to Labour in the mid-Eighteenth Century', *Economic History Review*, 2nd Series, 11, No. 1 (1958–9), 35–51.

A. W. Coats, 'Economic Thought and Poor Law Policy in the Eighteenth Century', *Economic History Review*, 2nd Series, 13, No. 1 (1960–1), 39–51.

Alun C. Davies, 'The Old Poor Law in an Industrialising Parish: Aberdare, 1818–1836', *Welsh History Review*, 8, No. 3 (1977), 285–311, shows the welfare side of the Old Poor Law in action.

Sir F. M. Eden, *The State of the Poor* (three vols, London, 1797), now available in facsimile, and full of illuminating information on parishes throughout England.

M. W. Flinn, 'The Poor Employment Act of 1817', *Economic History Review*, 2nd Series, 14, No.1 (1961–2), 89–92.

E. M. Hampson, 'Settlement and Removal in Cambridgeshire, 1662–1834', *Cambridge Historical Journal*, 2, No. 3 (1926–8) 273–89.

E. M. Hampson, *The Treatment of Poverty in Cambridgeshire, 1597–1834* (Cambridge, 1934).

D. Marshall, *The English Poor in the Eighteenth Century* (1926).

D. Marshall, 'The Old Poor Law', *Economic History Review*, 8, No. 1 (1937), 38–47.

J. D. Marshall, 'The Nottinghamshire Reformers and their Contribution to the New Poor Law', *Economic History Review*, 2nd Series, 13, No. 3 (1960–1), 382–96.

E. W. Martin, 'From Parish to Union; Poor Law Administration, 1601–1865', in E. W. Martin (ed.), *Comparative Development in Social Welfare* (1972), 25–56.

M. D. Neuman, 'A Suggestion Regarding the Origin of the Speenhamland Plan', *English Historical Review*, 84, No. 331 (1969), 317–22.

M. E. Rose, *The English Poor Law, 1780–1930* (Newton Abbot, 1971).

P. Styles, 'The Evolution of the Law of Settlement', *The University of Birmingham Historical Journal*, 9, No. 1 (1963), 70–123.

W. E. Tate, *The Parish Chest* (Cambridge, 1946).

Index

55